DEDICATION

To the creation energy that is in everything and in everyone, to all the traveling entities of this galley towards the unknown and the opportunity to be in this new time, in this moment of great rebirths of a spiritual life.

FOREWORD

The flowers are always beautiful because they are always naked; and also, if humans learned to undress the reality of these illusions that hides the essence would equal them.

But few are the seekers of cosmic beauty; prefer to repeat the old songs, and tell the old stories than go beyond monotony, the automation and the perfect conditioning of the spirit.

So, the sons of light are lost in time in the midst of mental darkness, because are valuing the reality makeup, elaborate to "fill in" the voids of the soul.

Therefore, by magical moments, this divine entity begins to express with these limited words what there is beyond the veil. Thus, all existence is naked to raptureing the creature with the creation energy.

Wherefore the men that are awake will travel in parallel universes for a cosmic orgasm with the primordial atom, and those that are sleeping will continue in the world of unreal dreams.

Then, with the approximation of these changes, many questions arise in rural and urban areas, triggering psychic shock to alert these humanoids and make them grow to see beyond their navel, which drags from birth, the constant creative force everywhere.

So In a splendorous rebirth of the primitive womb, a new entity will begin to live a UNVEILED REALITY.

Shakti

INDEX

MYTHS

DREAMS

ILLUSION

MEN'S PUPPETS

SEX VAMPIRES

PSYCHIC SHOCKS

RAMBLINGS

INSIGHT

RATIONAL ANIMAL

VOICES OF TIMES

GUILLOTINE OF TIMES

THE SHAMANISM

INSIDE ALCHEMY

LIBERATING FROM THE SELVES

SPIRITUAL EXODUS

FEAR

FEAR OF PLEASURE

PASSIONS

MONOTONY

FREEDOM

HUMANOID

DEATH INSTINCT

DIE OR BEAR AGAIN?

DIE IS TRANSFORM IN

SPIRITUAL MONOPOLY

THE VULTURES WHO TRADE JESUS

THE NUN OF A NEW AGE

SACRED PLANTS

SAINT "DAIME"

A SHEET OVER THE GRASS

INSIGHT MOMENT

On the ridges of the silent mountains of the world
the man was enthralled in deep thoughts
in search of the contained answer,
in the intrinsic conductive soul of life.

Then, this integral entity has his expanded consciousness,
and living tuned to high frequency;
so, enters and leaves the invisible dimensions
enriching the spirit with new visions.

So, the spirit is free from programming to possess
understanding the beauty of these changes;
and while contemplate the mystical horizon in transformation
he finds himself in the source of rationality.

Then, full of natural knowledge
tune with the original energy;
dancing the music of creation
celebrate God in a prayer.

EVERYTHING IS ENERGY

In this time of the light consciousness expanded;
discovered his spiritual code in an essence that smiled
to see the smart sparks swirl in the air
and there manifest the universal energy of the divine pulsate.

In the microcosm and the macrocosm are all entities;
so the invisible life is the same as the visible with different
forces
full of strength to be the plasm of luminous thought
in this infinite age of radiant shine.

This to be reborn every morning of the sun radiating
show the man that he was like this one day;
today he learned from the rays to overcome the dimensions;
so, he understood the whys of the creations.

An eternal revolve around the core creator
the entity becomes deified electrons, becoming his own Lord;
free creative energy and creature,
eternal participant of this holy madness.

Sparks of primordial Atom,
propagating the original ethereal fluid
these are souls, daughters redeemed by wisdom,
in full alpha state with the intangible if ecstasy.

MYSTICAL MAGIC

In the transcendentality of the fragile entities of "gaia"
if blends with the obscure silhouettes of "maya"
the subtle energetic forms of essence
newly acquired consciousness.

So, the intelligent spark if liberate from the creator fire;
it twirl inconstantly and glide like the "condor",
and, in the timeless state, travels in infinite dimensions
celebrating the fullness of the free son of the creationist light.

Then, in the conditioned life or in the free life,
rejoice the atom with the magic found
from the morning dew drops on the leaves of yams,
to oceanic love and by the creative force that integrates this
life.

But the return is inevitable to the womb of magical light,
so, vibrates the subtle light bodies with magnetic waves;
to interconnect in cosmic orgasm and expand consciousness,
and delighted with these conscious atoms tunes out with the
primordial energy.

Therefore, the soul enters into communion with pure energy
before the "Big Bang",
losing the individual consciousness and integrating into the
sweet madness;
and now is again in the original cradle of the cosmos
with all the adventures in the backyard of the Supreme.

THE ILLUMINATION IS AT THE MOMENT

The consciousness that has not yet awakened to this eternal return
Becomes repetitive puppet controlled by habits;
then, these infantile actions before the hidden truths of infinity,
causes the entropy of this entity that sleeps on the divine altar.

However, if, during your breathing, you perceive the full soul inside yourself,
you wouldn't have to beg, only enthrall with the existence,
but how can you not connect with the inner whole, you lose the peace,
then, pass the earthly experience, plunged into the illusory world of inferior dimensions.

And lost in illusory labyrinths, projected by the deteriorated mind,
reintegrates in the moment in syntonize with the irrational animal of the "Sahel";
acting like a wild beast from past lives,
show themselves as human metamorphoses with mad souls.

So this aberration of the sons of light, make the entity to live another story;
letting escape the magical instant of the "Quantum Leap"
disconnects the possibility of experiencing the cosmic ecstasy,
representing the medieval characters in this illusion of being alive.

So goes the traveler of the stars confusing the windmills with the dragons,
in search of the encounter with yourself not to be lost in this cosmic path
on the Earth that also grows slowly.
Everything would be resolved if the spirit would light up and see its way into the multiverse.

But consciousness is trapped in this terrestrial holography,
So, consciousness can not perceive the possibilities in the now to get out of this bubble,

remaining in a cycle of births and deaths on this "samsara" wheel,
and then does not free itself from the existential illusion of this third dimension.

But all consciousness that comes back to itself to get rid of its projected illusion,
and will depart to other timeless dimensions distant this holography,
transubstantiating with the divine sparks in the midst of dark energy;
for a rearrangement of the quantum super strings to new possibilities of existence.

THE SPIRITUAL QUEST

The latent essence awakens to the real world,
but is unable to transcend the illusions of everyday life;
these institutionalized dogmas by the mechanicity of
existence,
illusory conventions to trap the soul in its mental projection.

But the restlessness present in the nucleus of this conscious
atom,
makes the living a seeker of the transcendent invisible;
then in desperation to appease the inner world,
the consciousness passes through all religion and only finds
confusion.

Therefore these false creators of the sects that use of the pain
and the fear,
to condition believers who believe in any plot,
all will be lost in their religious lies,
but they will not prevent the truths from expressing themselves
in grand minds.

So, that one who seeks God will find him everywhere;
and this interaction with the divinity will unify;
as part of the primordial energy consciousness will expand
infinitely,
finding, finally, the reason of all creation.

Thus, without soul, without spirit and without carnal body,
consciousness will be just a cluster of intelligent atoms in the
astral;
and free from physical laws delights with superior intelligence,
in a full cosmic orgasm in this transcendental contact.

PARALLEL UNIVERSES

Paying attention to the existence of heart beats
this temple generator of the divine song
makes man a conscious thinking animal,
predisposed to open invisible wandering paths,
toward the parallel universes.

So, In the spontaneity of the steps on the coagulated light,
one can perceive the interrelation of these spiritual journeys;
and following the intuition of the shamanic ancestors,
the spirit enters into communion with its essence,
finding the truth of mental projections in the sacred
archetypes.

Therefore, it is naturally connected with the time of this new
era,
and the entity loses itself in daily life and begins to inhabit the
various multiverse;
so, discover the simplicity of living natural,
the harmony sought in all lives and even in the astral,
thus, the entity makes its morning prayer and tells its story to
the universal atom.

Reconnected to original source,
the spirit delights in spiritual pleasure;
without any ritual finds the sense of each step,
the cry, the smile, everything necessary for this great compass
from creator to creature, metamorphosed into a single
sculpture.

Therefore, the primitive universe was found;
God has also been Son, Father and Mother; now is modified;
became the synthesis of your creation,
and telling the creatures all the adventures of the heart,
then, there is a cosmic catharsis, expanding the
consciousness of all lives.

UNVEILED REALITY

The third vision unveils the fictional reality;
The veil that covered the enigmatic faces of the truth
to unravel the mystery of the creation,
which has evolved in all lives to harmonize in this new era of
adventure.

So, open is the conscience of man, son of the divine essence,
expanded the knowledge rejoices with the understanding of all
the experiences;
and the creationist energy shows itself in the experiences of
all moments;
thus, the entity finds the reason of its existence when
contacting the magic of the complete rebirth.

Therefore, there is only celebration for the discovery of this
new heart;
the inner God begins to pulse in the mind with emotion;
and full of the creationist energy,
the entity reborn from the ashes and feels like a "condor".

Thus, freed from the illusion, which had as real,
It experiences the cosmic spiritual pleasure;
and dancing to the sound of the song of destiny,
recalls and relives all past lives when the spirit was just an
atom without a north.

Then, integrated into this new way of seeing the unknowable,
the soul stays on alert to perceive the invisible,
and so, the soul can tell her story to the traveling sons of the
multiverse,
which they will perceive to be the very extensions of God.

EVOLUTION

The human with clothes differs from the animal,
but its essence brings memories of the ritual,
when coming down from the trees to the ground;
to live in the caves as a conscious atom,
and have multiple orgasms with females at their disposal.

Thus, came humans to populate this terrestrial holography,
and tribes were led by hybrid "Orion" entities,
then, the "Orion" entities brought the fire and began the
conflict for power,
they divided the planet and created the borders.

In this way the wars did not end,
and the humanoid struggles for the illusion of possessing the
images of his mind.
So, in contemporary times still fighting for ghost photons,
in an eternal illusion of possessing the various faces of
quantum superstrings.

But hunger, death and the imprisonment of the soul in the
body,
causes a spiritual entropy in this divine energy.
Being that this degeneration of this creature of the caves,
we always observe unbalanced behavior in human relations.

Therefore, the divine essence was lost,
love for one's neighbor was like a shadow in "Platão" of cave;
and the evolutionary cycle has its end in this age,
when disconnected is the conscious atom of the quantum
vacuum.

PRISONER SOUL

In the complex rearrangements of the quantum superstrings,
the soul becomes restless and suffocated, imprisoned in the
physical body,
by being in tune with the vibrations of the primitive atoms,
these points of intelligent light travelers timeless toward
primeval energy.

So, sometimes the soul gets lost in the way in its mental
projections;
but nothing is in vain, for he learns at every step on this road
of knowledge;
and when the essence learns to return to itself it knows the
liberation,
then, the free spirit searches in other multiverses for new
connections.

But the soul has to return as long as it is imprisoned in this
terrestrial holography,
because it is connected by the thin thread of light of the
singular arrangements of the "Higgs Bosons",
so, it returns the prison of the physical body with dense matter,
and already begins to feel the agony of this imprisoned.

In this way the consciousness of these intelligent atoms
becomes saddened,
and the body is subjugated by the fear learned in this
repressive culture,
then, wounds are opened by cellular memory,
but everything is part of this epic path of conscious light.

What, then, is this thinking energy, which sculpts itself at all
times?
Will it really be a trapped soul or an expression of the various
divine faces in playful atoms?
Therefore, without remembering of the various adventures in
other dimensions the soul walks without north,
until realizing in the way that the direction for freedom is the
return to itself.

TIME GUINEA PIGS

The reason has come to inhabit the mind of these human
hybrids sons of "Orion",
but the emotions of primitive man remained in the basements
of the modified mind;
so, the mind sometimes expands or contracts in emotional
possibilities,
and at the core of the guinea pig the essence has the intuition
that it is not only this biological machine.

Thus, believing in this holography elaborated in alien
laboratories,
the terrestrial entity makes its walk without any awareness of
its birth,
and always vibrating in tune with the dense matter of involute
dimensions,
the guinea pigs of the time are distracted with the mirrors left
by the gods of "Orion".

But there are still some rare moments of intuition,
when the soul comes back to itself for clues of the way.
So, the atom begins to investigate itself to know its origin,
and even surviving with the fragmented soul the biological
machine moves toward the light.

The entity under construction is modeling itself every day;
this way they sometimes confuse the windmills with dragons;
but at other times with the goal of expanding consciousness
the spirit is constantly in focus,
therefore, the earthly experience passes through the birth and
death of the biological body.

Thus the entity searching for new possibilities goes through
several experiences,
and sometimes they do not perceive the illusion of the social
roles they represent;
this way interacts with the shadows of the caves thinking they
are intelligent,
and believe in these mental projections as if they were real
things.

But behind this northless entity has the dark energy that
makes it move far beyond spiritual entropy,
and the saga of this transcendental adventure moves the soul
to the return to primordial energy;
in a return to discover the source of consciousness of these
intelligent atoms,
so, entities may at another time with the expanded
consciousness create other lives.

3rd MILLENNIUM

At the threshold of this uneasy age,
afraid of the end of this village,
the entity flees to the bush
trying to get back to a new birth.

Aborted in time by religion,
never learned at least forgiveness,
now, run aimlessly and with pain
to be sucked by the sanitizer planet.

The cycle of gross matter ends,
remaining only the hybrids men with expanded
consciousness,
with the best feelings inherited from the sons of "Orion",
for a new human interaction on the transformed Earth.

Now all the races will be found,
without borders they will gather in the squares.
They will speak of the vital energy,
and also of the creator, of the creature, and the things of the
astral.

REAL HALLUCINATIONS

In the mental labyrinths of modern men,
thoughts parade like ghosts of past lives
in characters such as kings, pariahs and medieval inquisitors,
thus, these entities become confused before the various
possibilities of existence.

Unbalanced are the creatures,
for not understanding the beyond of this mechanicity;
due to so many mysteries accumulated since other past lives,
entities believe that cave shadows are intelligent
consciousnesses.

Consequently, deluded by the paradoxical actions of nature,
so, they sleep in this dimension in a spiritual entropy.
And every day they intoxicate their essences with contact in
the astral,
confuse the real with these holographs of various dimensions.

But penetrating into the primitive womb of the mother-
goddess, creator and creature,
these intelligent conscious atoms seek a referential,
because lost in the chaos built, thinks to have been born of a
sexual organ,
while in reality they have emerged from the creativity of
quantum superstrings with dark energy.

In the energy that caused the "Big Bang" there was already
the duality in these entities that arose;
the concave and the convex were connected in the primitive
orbits;
emerged the plurality of the entities with their interactive
minds,
populating the entire universe and making yourself in each
moment in various dimensions.

INSIGHTS

In the silence of the night,
play the shadows of humanoids
tea drinkers of the "Saint Daime".
These primitive rudderless travelers
go to the world of the initial forms
seeking the guardians of other dimensions,
in all the timeless possibilities,
the answer to the conflicts
of the domineering ego
the cause of pains
of the spirit, still prisoner
from the clutches of this gondolier
that leads and brings the self
for the altar of this atheist,
believer in the God of the vegetable,
this living energy in the original mind.

PAST LIVES

Heir to the beast that was in the initial era,
left in the man, in his subtle body, the primordial message;
load the mental habit in the act,
when howled in lugubrious woods of Tahiti.

The living humanoid wolf,
reacts instantly when he hears the chords
of the animalistic sound contained in the heart,
starting to act without emotion.

Brutalized in the way of treat,
brings the old habit of mistreat
all entities aware of themselves,
those freed from the future.

But the soul rooted by civilized barbarism,
kills every day the free think in this industrialized era,
thus, passing from animal to computerized machine;
this is the end of yet another human adventure in this time of
technological advancement.

RESTLESSNESS

Distressing moments of the last search of the original self,
makes the creature despair of the need to find oneself,
and the insecurity of the way makes the stingy andante in
thought,
losing, in the moment, the perception to enter the real world.

In this spiritual sterility if discussion with the carnal body,
these "Higgs Boson" do not know how to balance the energy
of the libido,
for they also want to be part of the adventure of the spirit,
but in this mindless contest of body and mind both are lost in
the dogmas of this dimension.

Then, in this daily illusion of this terrestrial holography,
the soul loses the cosmic rhythm and troubles the heart,
not knowing where to walk collects alien egos without emotion,
thus, the entity loses its time in the illusion of believing in the
images that its mind designs.

In this way this conditioned consciousness brings back in its
cellular memory all the dogmas of the past,
and before the other what he sees is only his projected image;
then, the soul rushes out of its unconscious projection,
therefore, it is frightened by the aberration of this found
dimension.

In this human adventure of eternal search
by the lost identity, when he challenged the creator,
wander that forgotten entity full of pain,
because he has not yet found the antidote that will cure him.

All mankind creeps into a deadly silence,
and predicting your own annihilation,
imagines miraculous leaks before shutdown,
and in panic controlled by science dulls the spiritual essence.

THE FEAR OF THE END

The legend of inherited eternity,
makes the humanoid dream of other dwellings,
seeking relief from existential conflict,
of the millennial ghost, resident of a carnal body.

In fear of the end, the mind is eternalized in the moment,
fantasizing in time its prolongation,
and desirous of transcending the now,
travels in the psychedelic revolutionary ideas of this last hour.

In the awakened world of cosmic timelessness,
slide the thoughts on the tentacles of the magnetic forces,
these creationist lights of early consciousness,
missionary conductors for high vibrational frequencies.

In the eternalizing mirage of the divine spark,
remain in deep samadhy in the astral,
hibernating the vital energy until the return to the sacred
womb,
to celebrate the birth of expanded consciousness.

There are so many miraculous intellectualized inventions,
used by thinking energy to avoid being eliminated,
getting lost in their fictitious spiritual theories,
cry and call out the invisible the continuity of vital energies.

HUMAN COMEDY

The wandering passengers of Dante's Inferno,
populate the minds of the shadows, believers in the Bacchae,
bacchus is remembered but not experienced,
conditioned was the man following paths already known.

These common breeding rabbit entities,
those who eat, drink, have sex and act as lords,
but unconscious they are of the freedom of the enlightened,
because sleeping through the ages are always imprisoned.

Believing in the mirages of the human reality,
forget their divine origin to believe in this humanity,
becoming slaves of themselves and of beliefs,
survive with the prejudices taken as a sentence.

Misled by the road with its perfect artificiality,
feel eternal in any endeavor,
but are disappointed by the time annihilator,
the angel sanitiser, missionary of the Lord.

So are taken from the scene in full decay,
the poor, the rich, the good and the evil finalize the
experience;
the tyranny of these creatures is done in every age,
and the humanized doll always despairs.

SHADOWS OF GOD

Light appeared in the original world,
and of your shadow emerged this animal;
it does not know who it was, who it is and nor who it will be.
Walk aimlessly, seeking in your darkness the life that will
come
in the sparks illuminated from Allah.

Lost in the gloom of eternal choices,
does not know what to do with the world that lives;
because between the yes and the not, there has to be a
decision
by the opposite paths that lead to a corner,
in the unconscious asleep this hermit.

In the silent mists of the spiritual world,
the destinies of the shadows in the astral are programmed,
ignorant dark beings will be,
these specters of creation,
inhabitants of the land of promise.

Men dehumanized by the dark mind,
obsessed are behind their follies,
and become lords of the creator's servants,
give and take life in full splendor,
only to show their lack of love.

The divine face will be shown to the expanded
consciousnesses,
to make it happen to the work of the envoys;
there will be separation by spiritual affinities,
and the shadows return to realm of minerals,
leaving the light free for new journeys.

THE SILENCE OF GOD

In the stillness of the lost soul,
pray the essence deluded
by artificial makeup
that a silent God, coming from the astral,
placed on men-child
who live in eternal wanderings.

Alone are all entities
and, in the despair of being people,
try to talk to God,
where is he? Creator of himself and of consciences,
these solitary children, apathetic and sad;
will be the divine in heaven far away,
or here and now in the sick soul?

Oh! If God could talk,
not with the silence that is peculiar to him,
but with human words.
Perhaps a Latin father will speak germanic language,
to the baby that carry on his arms?
This detachment doesn't understand
and in the prayers we ask the supreme:
speak to us, Father, we esteem him very much.

We did not hear anything coming from there,
maybe the song of a bird,
or perhaps the incessant pinging of the wind
on fragile roofs, protectors for a moment,
of the man imprisoned of itself;
who knows God was speechless to see there
in the speaking entity the dark side of truth;
his naked consciousness act without equity;
we hope that no, on the contrary, there will be no hope
in the final harmony, in the search for the essence and in the
divine inheritance.

If the human voice echoed in the cosmic ears,
could be confused with those of monkeys,
such is the will to say everything,

but what he does is mute before the mysterious creation.
So, there is no dialogue in this generation;
unlearn to communicate with the silence of the soul,
and we began to call the echoes of our own voice,
as if it was God speaking to us.

But we are mistaken in believing
In mystics transcendental sounds coming
to unmask the primary cause of all things;
the silence of the creator is not a narcissistic mania in which
we think concisely.
But it is the way of teaching us how to learn again to listen
without deceiving,
the intrinsic language, coming from the heart,
without being incomprehensible,
and the silence of God will be, in effect, undone;
the man will then hear your voice hitting his chest.

BASTARD SONS

The desire to be beyond this now,
makes the spirit dream about other hours,
where you do not have to arrest yourself,
by makeup pictures of power.

With the essence liberated from the yoke of self,
would be a happy atom in the kingdom of heaven;
would sing Hosanna to the children's children,
this crowd that reborn every day without shine.

But the dream has not yet come to the now,
leaving the restlessness of yore,
seizing confused entities,
for not knowing what to do with this cocoon without use.

The melancholy soul grieves with the future,
and question the dead God who still lives within himself:
"Why is the soul in this life of fugitive bastard son of before?"
His voice is muffled by the mind that lies at every moment.

Embarrassed by life, the creature cries,
and nothing comes as threatening caricature
of the repressive father, creator and creation,
since the time of "Eve and Adam".

THE SELF OF EACH HUMAN

These illustrious guardians of the body,
interpret in the memory of this age,
the pluralities of this movement of all ports;
on these ghost paths that err.
The unsuccessful experience finds no hiding place;
succumbs with the sequels left by the attempts,
the construction of the perfect donkey hermit.

Be just zombies believers in the omnipotent,
make the pilgrims without soul go crazy,
to see the constant end of these impotent men,
miserable patients; they never realized the dawn;
figures displaced in these different landscapes.
From the initial world come playing with time,
and finally comes to this point in which he has to face himself.

The seven faces of the fictitious selves
disguise wandering children, camouflaging the essence;
the true dead life within the body from the beginning;
the soul is silent with so much mental inhabitant,
for the dead pretend to be alive at all solstices,
the initial individuality was lost,
the caricatures of the living are confused in these deaths.

Between death and life,
we support the ghosts that disturb us,
far from the expected peace, already forgotten,
we beg the unsatisfactory pleasure on the way to the tomb,
deluded by the landscapes and instincts in this walk;
but this death reaper of the divine light,
consumes the representative characters of life.

DISINHERITED OF A SOLITUDE

Buried in the world of the living,
the man begins to howl;
lost his identity
since antiquity,
when he slept in the caves.

Absorbed in the sick world,
remains in an insane silence,
locked in itself and in the bedroom,
talking to the ghosts of this boarding school,
about the end of the pilgrim soul.

In the illusory projections of the mind,
man touches colorful figures of animal life,
and he sees himself in front of the sleeping place,
the distant world where he lived,
was a smart fox,
guardian of the little offspring.

In these conscious hallucinations,
the being happens to be not the entity,
confused in unraveling the truth,
then lie to himself because of his vanity,
in judging oneself as a thinking sage.

But day will come,
when the mind is set free
of the merciless yoke of the cloister body,
and there will be no more pain,
only the expansion of cosmic love.

While not coming to transform it,
the entity begins to pray,
a little celestial energy
to placate your bestial hunger,
nestled in the heart of the creature.

Only the despair of solitude remains,
disinherited was the citizen,

when he was thrown without a compass on Earth,
and was rejected by the journey brother
on these steep paths toward yourself.

EMOTIONAL APATHY

Indifferent to the pulse of the heart,
goes the walker without any emotion
in the spiritual emptiness of this age,
dreaming of leaving that sphere.

Seeking relief from his existential pain
in the cluster of cerebral atom
contained in the altruistic entity,
the transcendental energy of love.

In this confusion of meaningless life,
silently weeps the mind of the deceived,
by the image that covers the truth
of this currently unidentified soul.

Lost in the hubbub of voices from the past,
let yourself be guided by the shadows on this side,
falling in mental precipices
of people maddened by their material possessions.

FLEEING

Not being able to do
of life a free living,
unbalance the creature,
causing the entity to proceed without direction
in search of a path,
in which the soul can walk alone.

To this illusion of belonging:
to the father, to the mother and to the Earth which will be his tomb,
all this only increases imprisonment,
of this mind full of conditioning,
since our stay in the prison womb,
where the birth was the first attempt at escape.

Fleeing by unknown path,
the soul leaves asking everyone about what happened;
there are no answers to this peculiar act,
but maybe in a moonlight
find the solver puzzle
of this great lack of love.

And the soul without the compass to guide it,
then it only remains to flee from those who want to imprison it.
In this torment to be wandering,
suffers from the insecurity of continuing to fight
and, in the end, die without undiscovering
the cause of this eternal escape.

SCREAMS

In the eagerness to utter a cry,
the mind remains paralyzed for the purpose,
to make themselves understood by these people,
dumb walking in this land of giants.

So, in this meaningless life man is afraid,
awaiting a north which has not yet been shown,
by the silent gods of the infinite cosmos,
the bastard parents who omit these lost children.

And the despair of the common man,
notes in his unusual laments,
in all this mass of ordinary men,
these unconscious and alienated entities.

These monkeys dressed,
show in every moment their savagery,
in this absurd human violence,
on planet Earth marked by endless wars.

The unbalanced leaders of the masses,
impose their desires on these alienated;
controlling these conditioned minds,
with the media and mass culture.

MADNESS

The body, this walking prison of the soul
is being violated by senility
of these bastard sons foolish with age;
rebels boys old unaware of karma,
violators of subtle energies
contained within the lost soul.

The body can also be the cosmic temple of the soul,
but if you lose the referential with the original atom,
will remain in an unparalleled solitude;
and forgotten in the world of trials and atonement,
then, the body prays to the Lord, Lord of the wolves and of the sheep,
to rescue his sons and daughters from this torment.

Thus, not hearing the creator's voice due to mental imbalance,
entities wander without hope of getting out of these beliefs,
but seek to liberate the body from alienating thoughts,
and despite the spiritual imbalance,
the entities seek to find their north,
even when they are conditioned by the behaviorists of all institutions.

Thus, entities are disturbed by meaningless existence,
and they deny the beginning and the end of creation,
dying in the moment by a spiritual starvation,
the souls go crazy and start chattering to the wind
in the hope of being heard in the supernatural world,
for the possibility of finding the primordial source.

A DEAD BODY

In a moment,
Wanted the mind experience
all these events,
and learned that everything has to toil;
so, quieted for a moment,
but in the innermost chatter
ignoring a possible suffering,
which asked for a moment and expressed itself:
"Was the inhibiting fear;
came out of sideline and held
the soul anguished and without love;
the transform of the entity
was done with ardor,
and became a delinquent;
then, did everything madly
to end suddenly
with a projectile coming
of the father, your executor,
now, judge, punisher
and main actor
the drama of the death of this evildoer. "

CATERPILLAR OR BUTTERFLY?

Who is this being that has become a people?
Is he the son of darkness or incandescent lights?
The mystery of life is in the transformation
of a simple bud, from which he leaves the flower to grace the
vision.

Metamorphosis is present in every creation,
"Darwin" had already come to this knowledge with the theory
of evolution.
And this constant activity of creatures,
the various possibilities of "Quantum Vacuum" become visible.

Nothing is static in this existence of memories,
electrons play hide-and-seek like children,
and the creator atom, before and after these people,
observes and is observed by intelligent energies.

In this interaction of duality,
creator and creature Interact
in communion with a spiritual cosmic joy;
so, with this creationist connection happens to universal
expansion.

The magic of constant change energy,
from terrifying caterpillar to fluttering butterfly,
vibrates the essence when seeing the transformation,
of primitive sparks into the light of creation.

MYTHS

The biped came to dream,
denying the roughness of the look;
masks the mind with fantasy
of being this image that creates.

And the entity believes in its projected image,
so, lie to yourself not to wake up,
and thus, will not see the mental distortions of humans
in political power, in religious power and in daily life.

So, get distressed and disappointed,
with this modern slavery,
inside these crazy factories,
with these men trained and infantilized.

Thus, begins with despair or ignorance,
to glorify the quadrupeds without intelligence,
and kneeling with standardized reverence,
believe in all this religious hypocrisy.

Sacred are the animal brothers who do not speak;
while the wise owners of themselves cry
for not discovering the emotion,
and are surviving far from the heart.

Thus, ended the interpersonal connection
remaining the sickly temporal individuality.
Then, the mind projects its illusions
for the construction of these everyday myths.

DREAMS

Those who think they are alive,
they are only shadows of the mummies who raise with the
howls,
of the awakeners of the captive souls,
those who live on hillsides,
and they are begging every day for the survival of the fragile
body.

In the robotization of primitive nature,
daily wander these conditioned and inactive creatures,
looking for an exit from the animist vacuum,
these entities are languishing the individualistic essence,
In the silent fields of the Earth.

In the illusion of being coagulated energy,
the body thinks it can change the course of the story told,
by the conditioned minds of alienated parents,
that make of the children an extension of the desperate men,
in search of a meaning of the dreamed life.

Then, in the unreality of the fancy colors,
the body caresses with calloused hands,
the lives that parade in this unusual adventure,
looking for refreshment in the heights,
to appease the tormented chatter of the disconnected mind.

And now, invisible creator,
what to do with the dead life by this pain?
Not knowing who it is, why it is,
and get distressed because of this walking,
towards the distant and unknown world.

ILLUSION

In this ordinary life without light,
we do not even notice how much we sleep.
And valuing the superficiality of forms,
we become mediocre ghost men.

Frightened by these stunned souls,
the entity takes refuge in its unbalanced mind,
but is connected to the outer prison,
where the happy life dreamed turns into pain.

Deluded are the descendants of Adam,
the enlightening parables confused this generation,
and begin to believe in everything that gives security,
politics, religion and hope.

Sometimes the entity despairs;
remaining confused and sick,
sees the movies of the dead lives,
realizing himself always behind the door.

The entity never dared to believe in itself;
when entity was born entity was humiliated by the vizier father;
at the moment entity walks solemnly,
toward the maddening desires of the mind.

MEN'S PUPPETS

Like creator pendulums,
we mark time with clamor,
afraid of the dermis getting old
and thus, lose the soul in a crevice in time.

In this coming and going in the ways of the earth,
we get tired of walking alongside the conflicting father,
this Machiavellian human-god,
who made his son an impotent phallic symbol.

In the mechanistic movements,
we forget the naturalist world,
to survive the days in the factories,
manufacturing these weapons of war.

If the gestures were not architected,
by the master lord of the whole proletariat,
we'd be gentle in expressing,
and the "reichiana armor" would have to cease.

How difficult it is to be singular;
transcend the family monotony,
aborting the fear of living,
and seeking oneself to learn.

If the mother actually cut off the child's umbilical cord,
and leave the son on his rail,
so, there would be more joy in history,
and there would not be so much memory trauma.

Along with childhood characters,
cries the addicted child,
to be an adult every day,
to continue the unusual paranoia.

On the verge of total imbalance,
quiet the mind with the capital,
being sold the body and the soul,

by the amount of thirty currencies of the entrepreneurs.

SEX VAMPIRES

These vampires from the anonymous lives of the streets,
connect their energetic tentacles in these unknown
consciousnesses.
Having permission, they extract pure libidinous pleasure,
satisfying the demented ego of this mysterious millennium.

Addicted by the energy of suffering,
relax heavy cells and feel like a condor;
navigate the magic of stolen chemical pleasure,
but the artificiality passes, leaving only the solitude of a
desperate.

Always seeking relief in the body of the other,
to staunch the suffering of these children of
misunderstandings,
getting lost in lamentations when rejected by prejudice,
are miserable by birth and live without right.

Bandits of the libido are these unconscious bugs,
go out to meet any charm in the temple of these people,
penetrating the innocent bodies, take advantage of this social
impotence,
sucking pseudo sexual pleasure from pain.

Insatiable unbalanced animals,
crazy normal aberrations, state leaders,
contaminate insane minds with their fantasies,
impregnating all kinds of hypocrisy in the herds.

The weakened soul without the power of the creator,
usurped by the official evildoer,
loses the reason of existence and leaves collecting other
essences.
In this maddening vampirism, the soul deepens its existential
dementia.

PSYCHIC SHOCKS

And the son of man waits the last breath,
on the walk there are several warning signs to never give up,
even when the entity does not grow vertically,
passing to forget the teachings of sudden.

Suffering without understanding the moment,
revolts against the firmament,
and helpless is in front of the phenomena,
interpreting this moment as punishment of the demons.

Ignorant son of the divine virgins,
bastard, crazy in these offices,
learns from the suffering instituted,
for having inherited the wickedness of this race of stupid
humans.

As a child starving and helpless,
without understanding this confusion of this terrestrial
holography,
cries and smiles in a mechanical meaningless life,
waiting for the primeval atom to decide where to throw this
body without air.

Dragging the memory on this planet of illusion,
remembers the martyrdom of all the lives
from pariah to king; Suffered in the crucifixions,
today the conscious atom asks: why are these children of the
passions?

Crazy about so many ramblings without answers,
knocks desperately on all the doors,
but the beats come as a mute eloquent silence,
then, the entity remains furious for being a forgotten child of
the primeval atom.

RAMBLINGS

The restlessness of these final moments,
leaves the blind walker in interpersonal meetings.
Making biased judgments
disharmonizes the timeless orbits of the internal universes.

Undecided about the imaginary paths,
makes the accelerated mind draw unimaginable routes,
in the basements of the collective unconscious,
in the attempt to discover a lenitive.

Thus, the unknowable remains distant from these petty
pursuits,
and divine light transmutes into holographic stories.
The human has lost the connection with existence
entering into an eternal decay.

In this way, like mosses clinging to the cliffs,
the entity imprisons its soul in only one point in the earth;
forgot how to do the astral journey,
staying lost in this hellish world.

In these real hallucinations,
the soul is deceived by modern cannibals,
these religious vampires of all churches,
who feed of these alienated consciousnesses in this illusion of
the third dimension.

INSIGHT

The Sons of Cosmic Energy,
remain restless in fear of symbolic life,
inherited from extraterrestrial atoms,
these shamanic theorists of the stars,
the dead masters, however, alive in the essence
of the man who expanded his consciousness,
and freed himself from the dementia of conventional families,
the illustrious jailers, fetal conditioners.

These children are also products of the ignorance of their
unconsciousness,
which become port ghosts;
and they all get hurt because they can not leave,
staying in an eternal succumb;
they forgot the secret codes of the universe,
losing the innocence of the freedmen;
and trapped in the fantasy mind of the now,
come to believe in the legendary beliefs of the past.

In this existential dream, they lost their initial memory,
and inserted in this terrestrial holography, they discover the
illusion of the atom;
thus, in ancient times when life was unconscious,
only cell memory could access multiple past lives,
and in these various expressions of cosmic life,
in this incessant quest of the eternal;
the obstacle that had disintegrated,
and the light of knowledge in man was lodged.

But, the enlightened singular man,
can not perceive his inner god
inside his body temple that carries everywhere;
and without realizing the power contained in his essence,
this entity ceases to live the now by the hypothesis of
tomorrow;
thus, they die in all lives with useless illusory actions,
losing the opportunity to finally leave "Samsara",

and by this comes the end of a reincarnation with the whole fragmented soul.

RATIONAL ANIMAL

Identified as polished animal,
the man adorns the body and the soul with colored garbage,
making this natural animal an industrialized barbarian,
and corrupted by the inverted values of robotized
commanders;
with mechanical gestures calculated follows the mass;
human emotionally unbalanced,
which struggles to retain gold that is just colored atoms,
but that hypnotizes all those who are in deep sleep.

Then man is deceived by the glow that blinds,
and cover his ears to the truth;
remaining in the darkness that denies
suffer by the ignorance of his alienated consciousness;
and as a barbarically conditioned animal
follow the whistles of "Pavlov" without question;
but it disappoints with this existence when it comes out of this
holography,
because, the invisible world he feared was only his mental
projections.

All in vain for the dreams of the evolved quadruped.
Not being what he thought to be in the invisible
beliefs in the unknown fall to the ground;
disillusioned with the hypocritical truths of the parents
free from the sick emotionality of the vanquished,
and the animal, once lost in its instincts,
starts thinking in a spectacular way
revolting against existence in this eternal conflict.

VOICES OF TIMES

These words that echo in the mind
from every place, east and west,
are voices of time trying to tell the truth
to the children of yesterday and from all eternity.

Time is the divine creator of existence
and, never forgetting the ramifications of his intelligence,
sends energy with messages of knowledge
in order to make the being full of power.

Many pretend to be deaf not to hear,
but as a ceaseless hissing of the wind of the future,
will open up to the reality of universal consciousness,
all the humanity that is coming out of its mire.

Celebrating the connection with the divine creator,
humans sing in prayer the "mantras" full of love;
thus, the interaction with the soul of the world takes place
naturally,
entrancing the spirit in the reunion with the cosmic mind.

And in the harmonization of all entities,
the spirit interconnects with all realities;
so, in the inner silence, one always hears the voice of the
Lord;
only now has the heart opened to this promising kingdom.

All began to hear the voice of Allah;
thus, the human spirit found its north;
and with expanded consciousness grow vertically toward the
divine source,
realizing at each instance the realization of childhood dreams.

GUILLOTINE OF TIMES

Afraid of the unknown emotions,
locked himself in the known and left the other's hearts,
so, "Carpe Diem" was ignored at the height of vital energy,
and time was atrophied in the mind of the rational child.

He followed spiritual hypocrisy and got lost in the illusion
of the vain beliefs of the invisible from another dimension;
and indifferent to the clamor of repressed libido
spent the moments without experiencing life.

Thus, living from the frustrating memories of those alienations,
goes unnoticed the now and history repeats itself in this age;
and having the tomorrow as a possible reality,
abandons the magic of the discovery of the unknowable.

In this way, passing through the same known paths,
gets bored of not having grown up;
"Peter Pan" still dwells in the unconscious
of the sick men on this infantilized Earth.

Reacting according to the beliefs of the ancestors
believes in all the legends, myths and even the deputies.
In this way, the lies inherited from all these social training
make these men only representatives manipulated in this
terrestrial holography.

THE SHAMANISM

Since the eras of prehistory,
the shaman already interacted with the environment in which
he lived;
he spoke to the animals, the vegetables, and the silent stones;
everything was part of the great soul.

When the sounds of drums were heard,
the cosmic dance began;
the divine song lifted the shaman to the beyond,
to bring the knowledge of how to use plants and animals of
power in the treatment of men.

In these times of religious primitivism, inspired by the spiritual,
the being was interconnected with universal energy;
and in this harmonization with the cosmic heart,
he used clairvoyance, telepathy, and levitation.

So, in magical rituals all went into deep ecstasy.
When they heard the primordial sound, they rocked with the
dance of another world;
in frenzy penetrated into another dimension
and, in this world without reason, they perceived everything
pulsating in the rhythm of the heart.

The gods took the form of humans and animals
when they showed themselves to the shaman at crucial
moments;
in this informal dialogue of creatures and creator,
entities rejoiced over these direct contacts with the divine
source.

With his expanded consciousness,
the pilgrims of this ancestral life,
interacted in constant communion,
with the creator and his creation.

INSIDE ALCHEMY

From Paracelsus with his tireless searches
to discover the elixir of eternity,
until quantum physics which passes through the enigma of the
double slit,
these challenging atoms of the invisible dimensions,
walkers of the stars that find the secret of timelessness.

Matter became energy;
time has lost its limit in experiments with atoms;
the essence of all things is shown in the microcosm;
the creator power was unveiled by magic,
and, this, is the "DNA" of all the particles of the cosmos.

But within the downward man of restless consciousnesses,
revolution takes place in a magical transformation;
consciousness finds light in its expansion;
the entity begins to understand the inner alchemy,
reconnecting with the primary cause of all things.

So, consciousness is sculpting itself in this transcendental
encounter.
Connected with existence
going on to discover the beauty of life that begins;
the mystery of creation unfolds in the consciential world,
and unborn children already play within pure intelligence.

LIBERATING FROM THE SELVES

When the desire to finish.
From the dream remain only dead files,
and hope become extinct,
then, the selves will leave at this time.

Will not have to return to other dawns;
then, concluded the cycles of life when they understood the
hesperus.
And In the magic moment of cosmic energy,
the selves will perceive to be just phantom photons of a
holographic life.

Expanded consciousness begins to understand all the
dementias,
of the believers confused by makeup that eluded him.
And the alienated mind in the deceptive power,
it is a consequence of religious dogmas that only know how to
provoke pain.

Then, suffering will be forgotten,
and of the collective mind banished;
the liberated entity of the selves,
will go straight to heaven.

A new humanity will be Born,
in the distant stars of Allah;
and the essence will one day remember,
of the adventure lived in the solar system.

SPIRITUAL EXODUS

The conscious atoms began a journey beyond the double slit,
using quantum synapses through the web of life in the
cosmos,
seek new places to live in distant multiverse,
a place where these cosmic entities can expand their
consciousness,
to discover the secrets of their existence,
in a drop of dew on a leaf of yam.

In the final twilight of this dynasty,
the wheat and the darnel will be separated every day,
to comply with the treaty which read:
In the primordial source there are many parallel universes;
thus, the momentary pain will be transmuted,
for the peace of eternal dwellings.

The renovating avalanches,
will shake the earth with terrifying madness;
because the Earth will also evolve;
"pachamama" is finishing a natural cycle,
and the quantum superstrings of "Gaia" are formatting other
possibilities.

Such is the natural law;
all living beings seeking new reconstructions,
in new expressions of this magic, which is the consciousness
of the atom,
this divine spark that goes beyond its own limits of knowing
itself,
on this marvelous journey through all these transcendental
parallel universes.

The energies in this way become replicants of the primary
cause of all things,
will be blown by these gravitational waves to all the ends of
the cosmos;
and all these entities that come to this blue planet have
discovered the cave of "Platão",

but will not immediately notice in the holography that they
were inserted,
because they are still distracted by these phantoms photons
that shape the thoughts of humans.

The new stage of men will begin;
the great phase of the heart will return
for all those who made their own story,
and left recorded in the cosmic memory,
all human actions of expanded consciousness.

In this way all quantum synapses have reinvented themselves;
and "pachamama" connected with these "Higgs Bosons"
conscious,
opened new passages for parallel universes,
inside this cosmic structure called dark energy,
thus, the human soul will execute the quantum leap to the
primordial source.

FEAR

When the self becomes aware of its end,
the man begins to be afraid of losing the collected illusions;
the dreams will fading with the magic of time,
then, the entity will find itself naked in the midst of conscious
atoms of the various multiverses.

And the fear of the next moment makes the soul insecure in its
walk,
but the fear still continues from illustrious shadows;
these wandering spirits, ghosts of the creator,
in the form of conscious luminous atoms project the existential
illusion.

Too much solitary consciences roam the deserts;
distant from the primordial source observe the winds;
modeling the mineral in the primitive forms of their ancestors,
come to light at that moment memories of other wave
collapses.

But who were these manufacturers?
Of life, death, and howling wolves?
Far from this initial reference,
humans become frightened of being in these holographic
bubbles.

Even when the castaways in this "Sahel" of the soul,
children of the invisible will wander in this state?
The fear of never having existed comes to the surface;
have been only the flow of divine light.

Cries the light without body;
it is not what it thought it was when it was still only a scope;
disappointed with the truths of the astral,
it is extinguished in the timeless thinking.

FEAR OF PLEASURE

Against the energy of libido,
the spirit refuses to feel the unknown pleasure;
in fear of pain loses the magic moments of the human adventure,
spending the time in the fictitious tomorrow of possible ventures.

In the future, it will be that, program the entity;
while the dermis ages only pain knows this indifferent;
the pleasure is always left to an appropriate moment,
but this time never comes, then, cries the disappointed human.

In the life of exhausting urban hermit,
surrender to the castrating rituals;
it is taught to him that to make love is sin;
are absurdities spoken by impotent fanatical men.

Humanity should discover the pleasure of smiling,
in this transcendental exchange of bodily orgonium,
and feel the ecstasy of knowing the origin of self in the initial womb,
in the dark and pleasurable bowels of primordial life.

The breastplate constructed by the living to not interrelate,
makes of this, an insane sufferer, unable to dream,
and, in the conditioned life of daily routine, does not live fully;
so, forgotten in time, he waits only for death.

PASSIONS

Driven by immemorial instincts,
we corrupt the soul with sexual games;
with this pleasure which does not satisfy the conscience,
but the body then becomes addicted,
seeking in the flesh a portal to another dimension.

In times when one lived
in the forests and prairies,
there was no such contemporary rationality;
everything was done with innocence,
without guilt, without fear and without dementia.

Today, the animal has become a thinking being;
and lost its naturalness before the lovers.
Then, going on to fight with its essence,
became stupid human in his experience,
with the phantom beings of past lives.

Suffering for not understanding the various faces of
consciousness,
then, gets lost in the mental labyrinths of the collective
unconscious,
occupying the spirit with various entertainment.
But it is always looking for a reason for existence,
thus, reality is shaped by mental projection.

In this holographic world made by ghost photons,
the illusion of social roles becomes real,
and dying is the pinnacle of this existential fantasy,
just when the entity begins to understand the double-slit
experience,
then, the thinking atom is removed from the scene without any
explanation.

The remaining humans that port this portal to another
dimension,
continue their lives immersed in intricate false relationships,
these entities are unaware of their quantum consciousness,
so, they go through life pressing a button in any factory,

and latent quantum consciousness waits for this idiot to wake up from this mental illusion.

The human comedy thus continues,
and these talking dolls believe in the mirages of their minds,
ignorant geniuses created by the primary cause of all things,
wander the earth in a meaningless life,
simply because consciousness does not understand that it is wave and particle at the same time.

MONOTONY

Another dawn
come to wake the living,
to repeat the moments of demented son,
ignored creature from last dusk.

Get up, get dressed, make-up, finally, fantasize to live the
illusion;
rushing, hurrying, late to the factory, molding and being
molded;
work to eat, not die, and be a respected citizen,
being one of the born ones conditioned by the techniques of
training of Pavlov.

Encouraged to retain gold,
go to the schools to learn how to achieve power;
trained to handle words become a villain with knowledge;
in the daily competition they dominate with arrogance the
other.

Everything is repetition, since the connection of the genitals,
and childhood repressed by inconsequential parents,
to the confused adult, to be or not be the child of a lover,
to degrading old age, poor bastards with mental problems.

Where is the now of the mystics that confuse these a fool?
The robotic worker is one more alienated in this assembly line,
and, in daily mechanicity, follows any industrialized pseudo-
religious guide;
this one rips off his brain, his heart, and his sexual organs.

We are all walking zombies, repeaters of the scenes of that
moment;
unaware of the state of decay,
survive to die in the last act of this experience,
without ever having known the truth of his birth.

FREEDOM

The dream of breaking new ground,
it's paralyzed at this time,
when the creature lost the charm,
to be the adventurous envoy from every corner.

Imagination travels in psychedelic colors;
finds there pure energy and new values;
in the world goes to seek the unknown,
seeing the possibilities in the actions with the libido.

The body meets in orgasms,
and the spirit in the readings of "Erasmus";
both participate in the madness,
of the experiential paradox terminated by the return to heights.

Freedom is in the consciousness of being,
to stay, to leave, to die and to be reborn;
then, dying is the maximum transformation,
if it is done every day, for yesterday, today and tomorrow of
the next dimensions.

if comprehension were total,
every animal would be free from all forms of imprisonment;
thus, having an alienated mind clings to the known,
losing the opportunity to connect with the unknowable.

HUMANOID

The mystery of the conscious atom that has become a
speaker,
it remains an enigma in this existential connection.
In his incomprehensible murmur,
expresses the loneliness, the fear of being only a perishable
body.

Far from the primitive womb, in which it fed this spark,
the atom goes in a desperate career behind that which mirrors
itself.
In the creationist energy of the existing,
kneel down, cry out, pray the miserable living.

In this relation of total ignorance of his divine energy,
the son of the astral becomes a common beggar,
consuming the illusions of this terrestrial holography, becomes
a slave of the sleeping mind,
and survives with the beliefs of being the master of his
dementia.

Delivered on karma imposed by masters without faces,
follows the ritual of the species paying a supposed evil.
Powerless in the face of these elaborate plots in the eternal
dwellings,
it fulfills all the guidelines with its dulled mind.

Unconscious in this journey to the inconceivable,
it's guided by the hands of the invisible.
The stray sheep is again found,
and no matter how disharmonious, his return will be
celebrated.

DEATH INSTINCT

The man in the affliction of being prisoner of the emotions,
begins to lament the very existence,
reminding of his whole life without meaning in decadence.
Giving up to fight for survival, he begs to die in his prayers.

In these everyday attempts to kill yourself,
depresses when contacting the pain of loneliness;
and the man, the son of the divine, has actions equal to a dog,
losing the dignity, degenerates the secular spirit.

Crawling into a cement ditch,
goes the being lost in its irrationality;
communing with the shadows of youth,
man becomes anguish for not having lived the past.

All lost in this time, he concludes hastily and breathlessly,
if at this moment the consciousness woke up from his deep
sleep,
there would not be so much pain in this mind immersed in
illusion,
in this actor of several lives in this cosmic timelessness.

Then, he concludes the act; the crazed traveler,
he kills himself with his bare hands,
in the middle of the crowd in the middle of the street,
finalizing this pilgrim's journey in this terrestrial holography.

DIE OR BEAR AGAIN?

Suddenly comes out of the scene some living;
his annihilated body is veiled by these people,
who cries too much for not understanding the transform;
dying isn't ending, but the start of a new walk.

If there wasn't so much institution
hiding the truth about creation,
freed would be the brother of life and death,
and would not have to go through this unlucky ending.

Maybe someday you can dance and sing when the body ends,
not for the end of it, but to celebrate the spirit to free itself.
In the near time of the era that begins,
these rituals will be performed to fulfill the prophecy.

The spiritual world here will dominate perfectly,
and the new values in the mind will infiltrate,
transforming the world, barbaric and ancient, into a new and
evolved world,
then all mankind will have grown.

Everything will be only transformation;
the rational animal with its new heart,
now, he will understand the beginning, middle, and end of this
existence,
and the God who was far away, will now reside within man.

DIE IS TRANSFORM IN

There is no need to say or feel;
the entity has only to hear the cosmic sound when
transubstantiating;
see, the musicality of the transformed body
in the subtle light forms of this eternal starry sky.

The fear of experiencing this unique landscape,
it ends when the being floats in the spheres where it will live;
then, the consciousness will merge in the divine light,
and one day this energy will again be boy or girl.

The eternal growth of the children of light is made
in the magic of continuous birth.
Thus, it is capable of interacting in the creationist process,
this transcendental animistic energy.

In the adventure of these playful atoms,
rediscover themselves in moments of disappointment,
experiences of other cosmic times,
when the energies of the now was part of the primate bodies.

In the collective and immortal memory,
the divine spark dies and reborn,
molding in time the racial shapes,
of these illustrious transcendental beings.

SPIRITUAL MONOPOLY

The groupings infantilized by the spiritualist fanatics of the
Crusades,
these religious hypocrites who have imprisoned the souls of
the miserable from Latin America;
alienate bodies and their vital energies
for totally commercial purposes.

These vultures of the religions manipulate the brains of these
entities,
with the sins forged to imprison the minds;
so, they brainwash these children of ignorance,
transforming these people of this continent into eunuchs with
their neurotic patience.

Leaving life in the hands of blind guides who are said to be
sent from the heavens,
the human pays this intermediary of God to access his
spirituality,
to obey the institutionalized dogmas,
making the living only a trained animal.

Taught from arrival on this earth
to obey the invisible who never misses.
So, frightened by the lack of meaning in the daily work,
the entity does not understand why it fights every day to end
everything at any time.

Therefore the Pharisees went mad to control these empty
souls,
they constructed the fictional idols in order to deceive and
propagate their fantasies.
so, this spiritless mass wanders like human puppets,
and lost in this dimension are all guided by these religious
despots.

The spiritual path is in the hands of these medieval
institutions;
with their modern inquisitions they do brainwashing,
emptying the mind of all questions;

turning these entities into stupid humans walking towards death.

THE VULTURES WHO TRADE JESUS

In the last moments on the cross,
when Jesus gave his last sigh,
the vultures had already divided their robes,
using games of chance to subtract the Master's clothes.

Later his ideas would be sold:
In squares, houses, streets and factories,
and in the name of the greater Master:
Stole, alienated, killed, and misrepresented Jesus' philosophy.

Killed by the greed of power,
Jesus remains alive within him who believes;
but for the Pharisee leaders,
Christ is used as a source of profit for these religious
hypocrites.

Then, the religious leaders exploit the ignorant sons of God,
these catechists of darkness use endemic misery to alienate
these souls;
and using a moldy book full of myths and legends,
spread the hypocrisy of this world.

Without defense is the infantilized mind,
by soul vampirizers, owner of the industrialized religions;
thus, the unconscious people go as flocks to the churches,
in this way they escape from real life to enter the trap of
religions.

But in the new time that is coming, consciousness will expand,
the false leaders will sink into the abyss that comes;
and the singular being, a believer in the Nazarene,
awaken in this moment and discover the Christ in himself.

THE NUN OF A NEW AGE

In the millennial quest of the occult spirit of God,
the female enters into an institution of religious fanatics;
and in this lair of wolves disguised in lambs,
the nun of the new age experiences all forms of sex in this
religious institution.

But she remains disappointed not to find love in this place;
the restless mind shows her imprisoned energy,
then, rips the habit and flees to normalcy,
seeking in the world of illusion a refuge to his insanity.

Discover in the physical world of carnal men,
the energetic exchange of sensual atoms;
experiencing instinctive life,
let secular hedonism flow creatively.

The divine orgasm is experienced in this human act,
finding in the enjoyment of the flesh the pilgrim spirit;
spiritual reconnection takes place in the sexual outburst;
the daughter returns to the mother's bosom, who is also a
father, in the virginal world.

SACRED PLANTS

This green being self-sufficient grows vertically,
after entering the dark bowels of the effervescent earth,
learn from the inner darkness over the full power:
How to elevate oneself and the animal to the spiritual world.

The "chacrona" and the "mariri" stand out,
these beings of the light in the form of vegetal elevate the man
to the encounter of itself,
when used in rituals of connection with the astral;
then, new paths are opened for the expansion of
consciousness.

Always resisting the psychedelic delight of this energy,
shows the man his inner strength to the vegetable that is
testing him;
the purpose of the vegetable is to remove man from this state
of ignorance,
thus, this entity lost in this unknown sea will find itself.

Navigating the dimensions of the higher energies,
consciousness is carried by the spirit of the vegetable into the
primordial source;
connects with the primitive embryo of all creation,
remembering the generations of many lives lived in
communion.

In the interaction between animal and vegetable,
the humanoid grows by ingesting the food of the astral gods;
learning the cosmic magic on the altar of his regenerated soul,
the entity frees itself from the collective unconscious.

Traveling in the colorful waves through the territory of the
unseen,
the spirit was ecstatic to see God as color, light and wonder of
the conscious atom;
so, in this adventure through the current time,
the human finds in the sacred plants the channel for the
transcendental world.

SAINT "DAIME"

In the far Andean lands,
the Incas discovered the divine essence,
which showed the power of the vegetable in the "mariri" and "chacrona";
the channeling energy to lead man to spiritual worlds.

Then, the forces of light brought this magical tea to the Amazon plain,
together with the entity of the vegetable which leads the souls in the ceremonies;
in this way the natives, the rubber tappers and all the seekers of themselves,
drink the "Saint Daime" tea to connect with the entire universe.

In these psychedelic journeys of primitive consciousness,
soul-seekers of light seek beyond psychedelic delight;
so, after being tested by the vegetable entity,
the light of man will learn in the original world.

With expanded consciousness comprise all life,
of the sacred archetypes bring misunderstood wisdom,
for these fearful barbarians who do not want to grow up,
and evolve into the primordial totality of knowledge.

In the visions, in the "burracheiras", the entity finds itself,
surrenders to the fluids of power and begin to see with the heart,
all past lives pass in your memory,
and the future is shown with all its history.

The integration of the Sons of Light is done in this song;
raptured by divine Pleasure danced in the salon;
paradise is found in this communion of expanded consciousness;
thus, life is celebrated through the power of the vegetable,
which elevates the soul to the spiritual world.

A SHEET OVER THE GRASS

In the deserted grasses of cities that wear blankets,
the stranger covers himself with a crumpled sheet;
this extended cloth silences the groans of this poor wretch,
which is ignored by society, and this invisible social being dies
every day to pay for the sins of the bourgeoisie.

Those crucified without audiences,
social outcasts always forgotten in Sunday prayers;
they are excluded from the holy suppers of these a fool,
these hypocritical insane consciences living a false epic.

On cold winter nights, these socially excluded experience their
own hell;
in the summer, the nightmare of another crucifixion;
thus, follows the "Way of the Cross", this son of Adam,
homeless, no land and no food, this contemporary man
survives every moment.

Whipped by hunger that kills him every day,
this tormented soul goes through the streets still chained to
their past lives,
begging the bread that is not distributed on these roads;
and, in the loneliness of divine disinherited, it identifies with
the collective dementia.

This spirit concentrates in itself all the evil of existence;
it is a natural catalyst of this ruling class;
thus, this divinized walker survives in the collective
unconscious;
with this life in full decadence calls attention to a new
experience.

In a new time after the quantum leap of these pilgrims,
these phantom photons will have other formatting;
fully attuned to the whole existence,
the human essence will connect the attractive whole.

THE LUSITANIAN ANCESTORS

In the intrinsic quest for understanding
to live every day without reason,
makes paranoia express itself
in the mind of the human who refused to pray,
according to the beliefs inherited from lusitanian peoples.

Empty, without the primitive religiosity,
entities believe in the shadows of "Platão" of cave;
and the primitive gods, the myths and the sacred jungle were
lost in history,
together with the forest folk,
thus, these invading ancestors formed the cities of Brazil.

Crowded in urban zoos,
these nude souls hold positions in multinational industries,
thus, these bodies survive in white slavery;
and they all die as anonymous assembly line workers,
in this "Tupiniquim" country formatted by Europeans.

This generation which are children of the Lusitanians,
loses hope every year,
for the promises of the sons of the court,
only benefits the local oligarchy,
and the miserable mestizo remains in the peripheries of this
country.

The myths of that time of the colonization of souls and bodies,
return in the general fantasy of this collective mind,
of these people who inherited the fears of many ethnicities.
thus, the people do not venture into other squares,
and survive in the hope of a better life in a distant future.

AUTOMATED HUMANS

In these factories, which program these men into imprisoning
ideologies,
the entity is trained to become an automated human,
these workers alienated from assembly lines just push
buttons,
to roduce technological machines for the comfort of the ruling
class.

In contact with cold steel without enchanted soul,
there's a strange relationship of submission,
kneels before his creation,
and loses all freedom to the industrialized machine.

Unconscious of his mission is programmed without realizing,
which is deceived by the despots of the official power;
thus, as an automaton connected to the dehumanized system,
this biological machine fulfills its role of civilized citizen
obedient to power.

This mass of maneuver, exploited by the hereditary caudillos,
passes the time anesthetized by fear deftly deployed
in the mind, in the body of these disinherited children,
cloned entities to serve all entrepreneurs.

Forced to toil for the bread that does not satisfy the hunger of
the heart,
remains anonymous child without consciousness,
following asleep towards the end of existence,
without ever venturing into the essence of himself.

This reserve army awaits with servitude the chance to be
integrated,
to the cycle of modern slavery by the labor force of the
children of ignorance;
and prepared in the maternal womb with machiavellian
patience,
this carnal machine is ready to execute what has been
programmed.

THE FLOCK

Massified are the children of the indoctrinated
by religion, politics, and civilized behavior;
following paths already trodden they will scream in chorus
without any adjustment,
hoping to find a reason for this life without emotion.

Unaware of the exploitation of every social segment,
become alienated consumerists, controlled by some business
group;
afraid of losing the safety of routine life,
all obey the laws of oligarchies and always remain at the base
of the social pyramid.

This herd conditioned by the wolves of power
lives sleeping, or pretending not to see, the drama that will
suffer:
unemployment, inflation, corruption and total state
indifference;
always believes in a solution coming from the astral.

While obeying without questioning the authoritarianism of the
state,
misery goes on eroding these alienated men;
without action the citizen falls dead,
being buried in common ditch like an indigent.

In this way, the herd survived like stupid humans;
no sheep dared to stray, afraid of the predator;
and imperialist time has annihilated any possibility of these
cowardly entities,
so, without daring, the spirit repeats its entire history as a
failed human.

THE "TUPINIQUINS"

The Warlord that leads
the "Tupiniquins" of another era,
sons of Cabral, the Lusitanian;
exerts its tyranny year after year
to the children of the earth and of the landless;
thus, these men without the north and lost in the labyrinth of
capitalism,
catechized by the predator system,
by the greed of our uniformed doctors;
these "Pavlov" disciples who brainwash the population,
to condition this herd to serve the top of the social pyramid,
and thus, maintain this modern system of slavery.

Here, in this republic of corruption,
those who sow the field are slain in traps,
and buried as indigent;
those who survive are persecuted by landlords and become ill;
others elect for lack of choice this demented oligarchy,
who celebrate Bacchus every day.
Thus, these professional politicians celebrate the possession
of the country's wealth,
in this way the "Tupiniquins" at the base of the pyramid are
totally ignored.

Therefore, these indoctrinated people follow the path traced
by the despots of power,
all are imprisoned in beliefs imposed since the maternal
womb;
this human mass is the doormat of the colonels who now live
in "Brasília";
and the children of this people will inherit this new format of
slavery,
and thus, serve the multinationals of the empires of the
northern hemisphere,
these voracious companies vultures of compulsory capitalism;
without self-love, this "Tupiniquim" malnourished,
becomes a fugitive;

Withdraws from hunger in the hinterland,

but in capitalist crises loses employment in industries,
and goes in search of his dreams cloned by "Pavlov",
finding in this animal behavior the programmed death.
Therefore, these children of the hinterlands,
wander around Brazil trying to solve their ramblings,
to be or not to be children of this nation?
But these seekers of their fragmented soul,
meet with a caudillo in each institution,
and saddened to see this people forced to walk in a circle,
surviving in an alienated way and totally lost in the shadow of capitalism.

Surviving is precise. Live! Maybe someday...
These were the thoughts of the "Tupiniquins" who died in anonymity,
for all were exploited at work by the tyrants of power,
these traitors of the people who sell the country to enrich themselves,
so, empty the public coffers and send the money to the tax havens,
and within the national territory use corruption to remain in power,
being that always who pays the bill is the conditioned worker,
so, this working mass walks without awareness of this exploitation,
due to never having accessed health, leisure and education.

How much ingratitude to these "Tupiniquins"!
once free happy men, today, trapped in bars;
they come back every day for their house arrests,
unfinished shitholes that call homes,
then, they suffer from varying pains,
and, far from the nature that took away their heavy pain,
have to shell out money to buy the industrialized drug,
when the medicine is missing they die in the anonymity of the periphery,
away from the house of the ancestors "Tupiniquins".

In this way, these survivors of this warrior tribe,
of the various pitfalls carried out by bandeirantes and the great landowners,

being still repeated today in the "Candelária", in the "slums", in the landless and in this modern slavery;
thus, these social invisibles of this unjust society disappear in the midst of the crowd,
this anonymous and lost people, without identity and without citizenship,
these suffer all kinds of deprivations,
and always exploited by the ignorant elite of Brazil,
so, these people of power use this cosmic consciousness as a beast of burden.

Even the God of the "Tupiniquins" were replaced;
the shamanism that was at its altar
was put into the fire within his home.
Why did these european invaders impose these religions?
In practice the "Tupiniquins" realized that it was to imprison the soul and the body,
now they were totally acculturated by this alien culture,
all are lost in the infernal base of the social pyramid.

While the elite at the top of the pyramid are looking at the sky, the land and the sea,
always eager to transform everything,
and, so, to profit also with the nature, besides the man already tamed.
In this way these power hogs are always opening accounts in the tax havens,
and the white slavery of "Tupiniquins" without fatherland struggles to survive every day,
so, all these people believe in the social role of this human comedy,
trained from the womb to serve, they have forgotten the Inner God,
and in this way the people are guided to the altar of the sacrifice of the god of work.

If those "Tupiniquins" had been born in "Índia",
would be the illustrious starving pariahs,
but as Allah wanted, they came here
to be the landless, the unemployed and the drugged,
all marginalized by this class of creptocrats of power.

But the "Tupiniquins" who still survive,
they hope one day to live
with a full stomach,
and the free mind of years of daydreams;
so, they can be freed from the illusory existence,
and, with altered consciousness,
start the journey towards the universal atom,
then, integrate the primary cause of all things.

While this quantum leap does not happen the children of the
earth despair,
and seek refuge in all social institutions
in a constant struggle for the survival of body and soul;
every day these anonymous "Tupiniquins" are trained to go to
factories,
to serve this capitalist system, which survives by human
misery,
so, in this daily madness the life span in this dimension is sold
for a few cents,
and in this way these biological bodies with divine
consciousness are explored as human beasts.

Therefore, within Brazil there are several Brazil;
the world can not see the reality of these "Tupiniquins" when
they serve these contemporary colonels,
and in this land of carnival, football and "samba",
this caste in power rules with indifference these hungry souls
of everything;
the human mass survives with the state bread and circus,
and the oligarchy of power celebrates Bacchus every day on
the island of fantasy,
they are all celebrating the perpetuation in power since the
invasion of "Cabral",
being that the population goes to the modern slavery in the
industries.

Without physical and mental energy to wake up from this
"Kafkiano" nightmare,
these "Tupiniquins" domesticated by "Pavlov" obey blindly,

the sirens, the signs, the capitalist rules and the submission before the great brother,
until the instant that body becomes useless to push any button.

Everywhere the people are deceived,
in religion, in politics, in the family, until they become depressed;
end up believing in destiny traced,
and continues to carry the tyrant and the Liberator,
but in rare moments of lucidity,
the soul realizes that it is within a collective dream.

Then, the "Tupiniquins" are crucified every day,
in this country of the camouflaged Maharajahs,
and the children of these humans who form the basis of the social pyramid,
part are trained in the technicist schools to serve the state,
and the other party go to the reserve army,
while in the plain of the Central Plateau,
the merry hyenas govern in theatrical form.

Therefore, citizens of this continental country,
alienated by the state, they clone more biological machines,
to serve the noble colonels "Tupiniquins" of "Brasília",
those landlords inheriting the captaincies of colonial Brazil,
these Portuguese invaders who still remain untouchable on this republican throne,
managing Brazil as a big farm, with the big house, the slaves and the sugar mills.

Foolish and ignorant men,
cloistered are in the mediocrity of the little dictator,
they are betraying these pariahs of the fatherland,
and in these political positions negotiated in this Republic of bananas;
they withdraw money from the public coffers in suitcases and underwear for the tax havens,
and the uninformed population leaves the body and soul in the hands of these vampires,

In this way this people slowly die and watch the blood flow through their open veins.

So, these forgotten people in the middle of the road,
they suffer from a forced colonization of body and mind,
and completely alienated follow paths traced,
transformed into efficient biological machines,
so, survive without questioning any situation,
all these sons of the fatherland are in the hands of these despots,
enriching these few aristocratic families in power.

Brasília nestles the imperial birds of prey;
all legalized in power by the blind servants,
these grown children and all entertained:
By television, football, religion, the internet and mobile phones.
In this way all remain alienated and obedient to the command of the great brother;
thus, the "Tupiniquins" warriors of the time of the Portuguese invasion, today are effective domesticated workers,
all serving the heirs of hereditary captaincies.

But many flee from this pavlovian conditioning,
even escaping, the soul still carries the acquired fears of all institutions,
so, these men are lost in this collective holographic mind designed to obey rules;
imprisoned in these medieval paradoxes, the spirit remains in this existential hell,
all following the various levels described by "Dante in the Divine Comedy";
and so, these "Tupiniquins" lost the art of dreaming,
and they were transformed into the technicist schools to be efficient parts of assembly lines.

These abandoned children of "Tupã",
they are subject to all the vices of this sick society,
and they are also exposed to domestic stockholm syndrome,
because in relationships one is hostage to the other.
So, in personal and professional life are all failed,

while all this is happening, the "Tupiniquins" survive with the fragmented soul.

VIRUS

The invisible representative of death
penetrates all bodies
to show the fragility of the children of the flesh,
sick offspring, condemned to disincarnate.

Suffer the creatures of varying pains
caused by the tiny life that kills to live on this journey.
In the complexity of the microcosm, the virus feeds on the
giant body;
so, this tiny life and without consciousness of its existence
makes the man shut up.

Life within life unveil the soul;
both living in the same house see the end and alarm;
all sons, one day, they'll succumb to time;
the instinctive and the conscious will return to the divine
breath.

Moved by Heavenly parody
live the magic rituals of their ancestors,
and, in the habit of living every day, they program their own
eternity,
then, they think to be eternal in this earthly experience,
but soon they are betrayed by temporal tyranny.

The invisible envoy being, lost in his primordial barbarism,
fulfills the role of divine executioner;
drives the movement of consciousness to evolution,
contributing to displacing the human soul beyond this
terrestrial diemension.

"ESPERANTO" AND THE UNION OF THE PEOPLES

In the beginning there was the unique language of the heart,
but the biped transformed it into sounds impregnated with
passion;
each people confiscated the word for misuse;
conditioned the barbaric and childish minds without warning,
and had the power to command these thinkers,
creating the various forms of expressions throughout the
earth.

Languages multiplied in an instant;
the incomprehension reigned among these mutants;
there was separation due to acquired prejudice:
By color, religion, and forgotten pariahs;
began the wars of conquest for power,
spreading the tribes all over the planet due to lack of
understanding.

Then, appeared the universal language
to unite around one ideal,
people who were separated by not speaking the same
language;
then, came Esperanto, the new language of the heart;
all speaking in the same tone everywhere
from the land of fire to "Bielostok", the dream will come true.

In the third millennium everyone will understand;
humanity will understand this evolution of consciousness;
these humans will speak through Esperanto their experiences:
the individual, the collective and the various past existences;
a great catharsis will be done when the people understand
each other;
reborn as a phoenix will expand their consciousness.

"UFOS" ARE HERE

The fleeting lights, moon dancers,
they sail disguised above the streets,
observing the humanoids in their paradoxical actions,
computing the evolutionary degree of these a fool.

These fireballs, with alien intelligence,
bring with them the truth about ancient Indians,
direct descendants of a special people,
different beings, children also of universal energy.

They are coming now to teach,
and to rescue those who ascended to the preliminary stage,
for the earth which is also astral life,
wants to get rid of the parasites of the animal kingdom.

Disturbed is the ignorant before the unknown;
imagining, seeing the flying discs, gods or ghosts of
deceased;
these visions are fixed in collective memory,
making all generations knowledgeable of this interactive view.

By not being spiritually evolved,
humanity can not contact with these entities,
but these travelers are slowly approaching
for the final meeting of humans with the mutants.

A new era will be reborn from this union,
no more children of illusion, but of the light that comes from
the heart,
demigods will be the descendants of this energy,
and freed from all mental illusions contact these timeless
travelers.

A COMET FELL

When here arrived the mineral intergalactic
in primitive form of uncommon stone,
the planet shook its poles, but sustained this silent being,
and, it soon became accustomed to this great body.

Tuned to this universal atom compound,
with its timeless subatomic structure,
made the rocks in the sea, the everest in the earth and the
stones of the polished gravestones,
with pompous inscriptions in Latin from illustrious freed men of
life.

In this silent evolution of the Creature from a wilderness
corner,
fallen on live planet in full transformation,
come to awaken all molecular formation,
for the necessary evolution and then be able to return to the
primitive source.

Then, in this apparent chaos of the primitive earth,
from the stone that travels in time to an overdose planet,
in this way green atoms are born to flower the streets,
and, the naked earth is clothed with the colors of the moon.

Life sprang from the skin of that sphere;
due to the purposeful shock formed several craters:
which became the lakes and rivers that go to the sea;
therefore, the comet fulfilled the mission of colonizing the
Earth.

UNEASY RELATIOSHIP

And the son of the earth disagrees with the partner,
when, he has to share the misunderstood dreams,
by his uneasy, insecure and alien soul;
this energy from another hidden time,
living on the tyranny of the rational animal,
despair in the face of the faithful companion in the love that
could be lived;
therefore, in this relationship between hostages, the years of
relationship are thrown into the trash without mercy.

Unconscious of the superior force replete with the oceanic
love,
the sparks of lost light remain confused
in space-time; Seek in the other the secret of life without pain,
but the imbalance of consciousness in the process of
evolution,
brings a fight and an everyday misunderstanding,
then, emotional misery settles in these broken lives;
the poor living people crawl emotionally trying to make peace
with the heart.

As long as the secret of existence does not show itself,
the man will hesitate at every step,
and will not accept the love between conscience for being
afraid of being deceived;
living in function of various adulterated selves,
represent the fictitious roles imposed by society;
in this common life will not perceive the learning in the
relationship;
the earthly experience will only be a journey into the emotional
void of humanity.

Left to the mercy of their fate in these social relationships,
the consciousnesses within these bodies join with others for
this singular journey;
sometimes animated, sometimes discouraged, seek the
complement,
the man-woman connection at all times,
but the fickle mind dreams of freedom;

get rid of this castrating bond
to unveil their cosmic destiny in another reality.

STRANGE RELATIONSHIP

Without knowing what to do with freedom,
in its confusion the entity seeks a relationship
in an attempt to find a new identity,
and quickly leave his bitter solitude,
but this human spirit found only deceit and its imprisonment.

And now? Lord of the meadows!
your soul is in the hands of this unknown,
so, this relationship became a meeting of two hostages,
in this way the soul is confused and does not know what to do,
and the fear of returning to the solitude of the empty room,
makes this consciousness without love for itself.

What a strange relationship there is between reality and
fiction!
the dreamed life was no more than an illusion,
the routine takes over again,
and the human beast abandons your soul,
staying in this illusion of is living with someone.

The paradox of this mind that does not know what it wants,
make this existence an eternal walking in a circle,
staying confused not knowing whether to run away or stay in
this maze.
therefore, the soul grieves for having ignored the intuition,
letting fear program this earthly experience.

THE BUCOLIC SOUNDS

The Noises of Natural Forces
take us to the rural fields,
where water has fun in the waterfalls,
at the same time the wind caresses the stones,
and the birds singing in the trees.

Also the thunder is heard,
and, afraid of this sound of the invisible,
run the boy, the girl and the little dog,
these consciences seek a safe place,
and the mother of these children intervene: calm down! This is
just the sound of "Taiko".

Also the bellowing of the cows are heard around the house,
there is still the meowing, barking, and singing of the nocturnal
birds,
but the singing of the "Sabiá" is a singular spectacle,
this transcendental sound awakens the souls of this rural
environment,
and in this magical house, the sounds are shaped in
expanded consciousness.

And at night it's time for the owls,
of the ghosts also make their appearances,
the werewolf, the headless mule and the drover;
these are the forces of the collective hallucinations of this
yard.

But life also has to fight for survival every day,
because in this terrestrial holography the body needs energy,
and this biological machine is the house of the spirit,
so, this complex human is on this journey of knowing himself,
and in this experience in this rural environment he is ecstatic
to hear all these melodies.

Therefore, the soul is gathering its shards,
and at every sound heard of this primitive nature,
the "Higgs Bosons" transform into a cohesive particle and
filled with divine energy,

then, begins the process of rebirth of the inner God of each one,
to the great and expected quantum leap of the soul in this rural house of magic.

A THOUGHT OF A LEAF

The leaf fell...
On earth it disappeared...
Came back to new possibilities
on the highest branch of a leafy rosewood.
Then, the leaf saw the whole world grow;
also the cycles of birth and death.
The leaf already knew about this transmutation,
because in another life passed through this dimension;
returned only to arrive
to the flower, to the fruit, and to the sea;
there it will become an animal;
thus, it will return to earth and bring in its cellular memory:
Memories that were already leaf, flower and fruit;
now it is this cunning animal.
Suddenly this primitive clone becomes man,
and forget what was yesterday;
kills the tree, the animal and itself;
then, this consciousness without body goes mad,
and totally dependent on a transcendent world,
of these invisible powers of the multiverse.
Therefore, these alienated believers
in all the myths and legends of this planet,
build their fantasies in these everyday rituals
in a meaningless life full of fear,
so, scared at every step by not trusting himself,
become indifferent men without the vital energy,
wandering the earth like zombies.
In this way without connection with the soul,
and unaware of the inner God,
suddenly it's just an atom on the moon. "